A. P. J. Abdul Kalam

Savneet Kaur

DIAMOND BOOKS

www.diamondbook.in

Publisher : **Diamond Pocket Books (P) Ltd.**
X-30, Okhla Industrial Area, Phase-II
New Delhi-110020
Phone : 011-40712200
E-mail : sales@dpb.in
Website : www.dpb.in
Edition : 2022
Printed by : Repro (India)

A. P. J. Abdul Kalam
By - *Savneet Kaur*

Preface

A person whose life is a treasure house of thoughts and feelings; dedication and determination is none other than A. P. J. Abdul Kalam, an Indian scientist and administrator who served as the 11th President of India from 2002 to 2007. He was one of the most revered personalities in our country. The book talks about the life experiences of Dr. Kalam right from his childhood. It highlights hidden facts about his parents, his town Rameshwaram, his mentors, ISRO, and more. The book also depicts the hardships of Kalam and his mentors who have helped to mould or reorient his thinking, thus changing the course of his life.

We even get a glimpse of his love for books. A few of his favourite quotes are also mentioned. So many incidents from his personal and professional life touch the heart and inspire everyone to move ahead despite many hurdles and hardships.

Dr. A. P. J. Abdul Kalam

"Never stop fighting until you arrive at your destined place- that is, the unique you. Have an aim in life, continuously acquire knowledge, work hard, and have perseverance to realize the great life."

-A. P. J. Abdul Kalam

A. P. J. Abdul Kalam

Beginning......

Avul Pakir Jainulabdeen Abdul Kalam, known as A. P. J. Abdul Kalam, was born to a Muslim couple named Jainulabudeen and Ashiamma on 15th October 1931 in Rameswaram, Tamil Nadu. His father was a boat owner and he was the youngest child among five children. Although he had three brothers and one sister, they had a secure childhood both materially and emotionally. His parents, Jainulabdedn and Ashiamma, despite their limited sources, were very generous people, and Kalam inherited the values of honesty, self-discipline, goodness and kindness from his parents. Though Kalam came from a large family, their kitchen fed far more outsiders than all his family members. He belonged to a wealthy family that lost its luck and destiny by the early 20th century. Abdul Kalam describes himself that he had short height and ordinary looks. On the contrary, his parents had good height. Abdul Kalam did not inherit their physical qualities.

In 1939, Kalam was only 8 years old when the Second World War broke out. There was a sudden demand for tamarind seeds in the market. Kalam collected these seeds and sold them to a provision shop on Mosque

Abdul Kalam's family

Street to earn an Anna, which was a significant amount at that time. His brother-in-law, Jalaluddin, would tell him stories about war which Kalam would try to trace in the headlines of Dinamani.

He was always eager to seek new information and was blessed with the talent of learning new things. Kalam's three friends, Ramanadha Sastry, Aravindan and Sivaprakasan, were very close to him. Though the boys came from different religious backgrounds—Kalam as a Muslim while the other three were from orthodox Hindu Brahmin families—yet their religious differences and upbringing did not stand in the way of their friendship.

He was a religious person and shared a good bond with the priest of Rameshwaram temple. He spent time with his father, who made Kalam see the world fearlessly. His relations with people of other religions have made him grow in a multi-religious and patient society with a positive outlook. Kalam grew up listening to the stories both from the Ramayana and the life of the Prophet from his mother and grandmother at bedtime.

One of the incidents of his childhood left a deep impact on Kalam's young mind. When he was in the fifth standard, a new teacher did not like Kalam, a Muslim boy sitting next to Ramanadha Sastry, a Brahmin. He sent Kalam to the back seat, simply following the social ranking of Muslims. Both Kalam and Ramanadha Sastry felt sad at this action of their teacher. Sastry wept and this had a deep impact on Kalam. When Sastry's father heard of the incident, he summoned the teacher and told him not to spread the poison of social inequality and communal intolerance in young minds. He told the teacher to either apologize or leave the school. The teacher regretted his action and this incident reformed him.

Kalam was well-versed in Hindu traditions; he learnt Sanskrit, read the Bhagavad Gita and he was a vegetarian. Kalam also enjoyed writing Tamil poetry. Kalam was very fond of (Carnatic music) M.S. Subbulakshmi respected doyen. The vocalist, too, had a deep respect for Kalam and often served him food she cooked with her own hands. They ate sitting in a traditional manner - squatting on the floor and eating food on banana leaves.

A life-long vegetarian, Kalam enjoyed the simple pleasure of food as well. One of his favourite

Abdul Kalam's school

restaurants in Chennai was 'Annalakshmi Hotel', which he frequently visited before becoming the president. He is said to have relished the *sambar, rasam* and *bonda* as well as his favourite dish *vatha kuzhambu* and papad. As a youngster, when he was placed in Thiruvananthapuram, he was a regular visitor to the Guruvayurappan hotel. The owner, Parameshwaran Nair, recalls how from 1975 to 1982, he served Kalam a very simple food. Every morning, he would take a glass of milk and two *appams*. For supper, he would have only two chapattis and a glass of milk.

Another memorable childhood incident was when Sivasubramanian Iyer, Kalam's science teacher, invited him home for a meal. Sivasubramanian Iyer

Abdul Kalam playing his Veena

was an orthodox brahmin and his wife was very conservative. She was horrified at the idea of a Muslim boy dining in her ritually pure kitchen. When she refused to serve Kalam; Iyer did not lose his cool and not only served the boy with his own hands but also sat and ate with him. He invited Kalam the next weekend as well. Noticing Kalam's hesitation in accepting his invitation, Iyer told the child to be prepared to face such situations if he wished to change any system. When Kalam revisited Iyer's house, his wife took him to her kitchen and served him food with her own hands.

Kalam was fond of saying, "For great men, religion is a way of making friends; small people make religion a fighting tool."

He was a nature lover and liked to spend most of his time watching the waves at the beach. Not only this, his love for nature was seen in his behaviour as he had very soft and delicate feelings because of which

Kalam's love for nature

his mother supported and provoked him to practice music and poetry.

Since Kalam's father was illiterate, so he wanted him to study well. His daily routine began at 4 in the morning and ended at 11 at night. Life was not easy for him as he had to take a bath before taking his mathematics class every day and his teacher used to teach only 5 students in the whole class and no student was allowed to take the class without bathing. The struggle didn't stop here. After attending his class, Kalam went to distribute newspapers along with his cousin, Samsuddin. Thus, Kalam earned his first wages, which gave him immense self-confidence and a sense of pride.

Not only this that the days were tough, but the nights also went the same. Since the town had no electricity, Kalam's mother used to save some kerosene oil for him to light up the lamps as he studied till 11 p.m. The house that belonged to Kalam is still visited by many tourists on the same street.

"Life and Time are world's best teachers. Life teaches us to make good use of Time and Time teaches us the value of Life."

- A.P.J Abdul Kalam

A. P. J. Abdul Kalam had great love for his mother. He recalled incidents of his mother in his childhood:

"During World War II, in 1941, it was a difficult time for our family at Rameswaram... War had reached our doors of Rameswaram since the cloud of war had already reached Colombo. Almost everything was a rarity, from food articles to other items. Ours was a large joint family. The environment in the home alternated between happiness and sadness. I used to get up at four in the morning, take a bath and go to my teacher Swamiyar for learning mathematics. My mother used to get up before me and prepare me to go for the tuition. I used to come back at 5:30 a.m. when my father would be waiting for taking me to the Namaz and Koran Sharif learning in an Arabic school. After that, I used to go to Rameswaram Road Railway station, three kilometres away, to collect newspapers. The newspaper bundle will be thrown from the running train to the platform.

I used to collect the paper and run around the Rameswaram town and be the first one to distribute the newspaper in the town. After distribution, I used to come home at 8 a.m. My mother would give me a simple breakfast with a special quota compared to other children because I was studying ad working simultaneously. I still remember an incident that I would like to share with you. One day, when all my brothers and sisters were sitting and eating, my mother went on giving me chapattis. When I finished eating, my elder brother called me privately and scolded me,

"Kalam, do you know what was happening? You went on eating chapatti, and mother went on giving you. She has given all her chapattis to you. Be a responsible son and do not make your mother starve." The first time I had a shivering sensation and I could not control myself. I rushed to my mother and hugged her. Even though I was studying in the 5th class, I had a special place in my home because I was the smallest one in the family. There used to be no electricity. Our house was lit by the kerosene lamp between 7 to 9 p.m. My mother especially gave me a small kerosene lamp so that I could study up to 11 p.m. I still remember my mother in a full moon night portrayed as a poem with the title 'Mother' in my book 'Wings of Fire'."

He was a hardworking and bright student but always remained an average one. He had a great interest in mathematics and enjoyed doing it a lot. His desire to learn new things never let him look back. The biggest support that he received, in the beginning, was from one of the school teachers of Schwart High School, named Iyadurai Solomon. Mr. Solomon not only made him realize that whatever we truly desire for do happen but also made him believe in 'faith'. Solomon shared that maybe sometimes parents who themselves couldn't grab the opportunity of education can always raise and encourage their child and change his life through the act of faith as it is only the faith that can change one's destiny. As Kalam was a nature lover, his cousin as well as his brother-in-law, Ahmed Jallaludin, encouraged him more to focus on nature's beauty and, along with this, developed a religious vision to look at the world.

One of Kalam's mathematics teachers once shared an incident with the entire school in a morning assembly that he once caught him loitering in the classroom and held him from his scruff. Iyer was confident that whoever he had been strict with became a successful person. A few months later, Kalam scored full marks in his exam.

His love for nature and science kept growing simultaneously. The flight of birds had fascinated him since childhood, but in his college life, he realized that he wanted to fly aircraft.

It was when Kalam was 10 years old and his teacher Subramaniam Iyer explained how seagulls fly. Kalam had a lot of doubts and, therefore, raised a lot of questions which his teacher answered patiently. Not only this, Iyer took the students to the seashore

Childhood picture of Abdul Kalam

to practically watch the birds and observe their actions and movements.

"Wonderstruck, I listened to my teacher, the man who, while teaching me about the flight of birds, gave me a purpose in life to fly!" Kalam later wrote.

"The bird is powered by its own Life and by its own motivation."

-A. P. J. Abdul Kalam

After finishing school, he took Physics at St. Joseph's College, Trichi. He realized that through science, his spiritual self-personality might also grow. Professor Chinna Durai taught him matter related to the radio decay of substances. Later, he was dissatisfied all over. He regretted having lost three precious years when he discovered aeronautical engineering. But he was happy that he went through Leo Tolstoy, Thomas Hardy and F. Scott Fitzgerald during his college years.

Abdul Kalam's College, St. Joseph College

Kalam's journey of education didn't end here. For his higher education in science, he took admission in MIT, Madras Institute of Technology, as it was the only institution in India which offered the course of B.Sc. at that time. Since he had a keen interest in Physics, Kalam opted for engineering.

He first witnessed the practical of engineering when he saw his father built a boat all by himself.

"Every day I would wait impatiently till I could go to the place where the boat was taking shape....slowly the bottom, then the sides and the hull began to form in front of our eyes....Many years later, I would learn how to make rockets and missiles in my work. But that boat coming up on a seashore, which would take pilgrims and fishermen back and forth, who is to say it was not important or momentous

in our lives then?" He wrote in his autobiography. Kalam's father who had no knowledge of science and education proved to be an inspiration for him.

Kalam's father Jainulabudeen Marakayar

Financial crisis and poverty have always been an obstacle in the life of Kalam. No matter what, his true determination to seek knowledge and to achieve his mission had always helped him. To arrange for an amount of Rs. 1000, his sister mortgaged her bangles to help him out. However, he was determined to repay the amount to his sister once he had clarified his scholarship at MIT.

"This is my belief: that through difficulties and problems God gives us the opportunity to grow. So, when your hopes and dreams and goals are dashed, search among the wreckage, you may find a golden opportunity hidden in the ruins."

- A. P. J. Abdul Kalam

During his years at MIT, 1954-1957, his goal became clear to him. But, the lack of confidence in his attitude because of his background was a bit problem. He didn't settle for this and decided to overcome his weakness. He gathered courage and took forward a step to interact with his mates. Since the class group was small and limited and there were around 8-9 students, the interaction became easier. Interaction with teachers and mentors was also not tough as it was not an immense strength. He was so passionate to determine his goal that once he saw two dismantled aircraft at MIT, he felt too happy. He would sit there observing every part of it. After his first year at MIT, he opted for aeronautical engineering as a part of his practical knowledge which laid the foundation stone of his professional career.

At the end of his third year, Kalam and four of his colleagues were assigned a task to design a low-level fighter aircraft. Kalam took the responsibility of designing the model while others took over the control and designing of the model. Prof. Sponder, an Austrian, taught him aerodynamics, Prof. K. A. V. Pandalai who was a friendly and enthusiastic teacher taught him aero structure, whereas, Prof. Narsingha Rao taught him theoretical aerodynamics.

After much hard work, Kalam's work was rejected by his design teacher Prof. Srinivasan, the then director of MIT. Srinivasan did not even lend an ear to his excuses. Despite knowing the fact that it would take a lot of time to reframe it and disapproving

Abdul Kalam's first flight

Kalam's request for the period of a month, Srinivasan instructed and ordered him to submit his design within three days, otherwise, he won't get the opportunity of scholarship.

"Look, young man, today is Friday afternoon. I will give you three days' time. If by Monday morning I don't get the configuration drawing your scholarship will be stopped."

Kalam couldn't respond to this as it was the only hope upon which his whole life and career was dependent.

Kalam, without any ifs or buts, started working out his project. He had mornings refrained from food and the nights went sleepless. On Saturday, he took just an hour's break and went back to work. On Sunday morning, since it was his last day to submit the project, he kept himself engaged in his work while he felt someone's presence in his room. On looking, he found that Prof. Srinivasan was glad to see him working wholeheartedly and was dedicated to completing his work. He hugged him affectionately and gave him a pat on his back. His words of appreciation were:

"I knew I was putting you under stress and asking you to meet an impossible deadline. I never expected you to perform so well…!"

"Climbing to the top demands strength, Whether it is up to the Mount Everest or to the top of the career."

-A. P. J. Abdul Kalam

At the age of about 26, Kalam achieved the degree of graduation and was then selected as an aeronautical engineer at HAL, Hindustan Aeronautics Limited, Bangalore. He was appointed in the engine department and was trained on radial engine-cum-drum operations and even learnt how to check a crankshaft. When Kalam secured his graduation degree at HAL in 1958, two of his dream employment opportunities were waiting for him at his doorstep. One was the job of the Directorate of Technical Development and Production (DTD&P) of Defense Ministry and another was a career in the Indian Air Force (IAF). Since he was in the favor of both, he applied for them and the interview calls came from both of them simultaneously.

To avail the opportunities, Kalam began with the first choice and visited Delhi for an interview with DTD&P but somehow was not selected for it. He gathered his strength and went to Dehradun for an interview. His second call opportunity was with Air Force Selection Board. But the deal here was again not up to the mark as the test conducted was not based on the ability to test his knowledge but on a candidate's personality. He was not selected since he stood ninth among 25 candidates and only 8 qualified for it.

After getting rejected from the second-best opportunity of his life, Kalam was disappointed. He visited Haridwar to take a bath in the holy river Ganga. He was strolling in a sad mood when he saw Sivananda Ashram and went inside. There he met Swami Sivananda, who at once read his mind and immediately questioned him about the cause of his worry and sadness. Kalam was surprised by the direct question of Swamiji and narrated his whole story. On listening to his side of the story, Swamiji advised him to accept God's will and act accordingly.

"Become one with yourself and surrender yourself to the will of God," Swamiji added.

Not only this, after hearing Swamiji's words he recalled what Kabir ji used to say-

"You must be content with the lot assigned to you by the God. Have faith and patience."

Sivananda sits by the Ganges

"If you fail, never give up because F.A.I.L means 'First Attempt In Learning'."

-A. P. J. Abdul Kalam

These words of self-control and accepting God's will comforted Kalam and relaxed his mind. When Kalam returned to Delhi, he was called up by DTD&P and was informed about his selection. He was given the appointment letter then and there and was asked to join the same post he had applied for. Kalam joined DTD&P (Air) as a senior scientific assistant in 1958 with a basic salary of Rs. 250/- per month. His joining here helped him recover his sadness and he passionately and dedicatedly worked in making aeroplanes airworthy. During his first year, he worked on supersonic target aircraft with the help of his officer in charge and received appreciation from Dr. Neelakanta. Lately, he was appointed in Kanpur and from there directly to a new set up of the 'Aeronautical Development Establishment' (ADE) at Bangalore.

Here at ADE, he began a new and challenging task. He headed a team of four people and opted to design and develop an indigenous hovercraft. The irony struck that all of them did not know anything about the design and development of Hovercraft, but their determination, enthusiasm and commitment kept them all together to work on the project. So, the work started from scratch.

After some time, may be about a year or so, his project was examined and surveyed by the then Defense Minister V. K. Krishna Menon. He was the one who

Readying equipment to be carried by a sounding rocket into the atmosphere are Kalam and R. Aravamudan

played a key role in setting up and the development of the Defense Research and Development Organization. He keenly observed his project and showed interest in checking up on the progress of Hovercraft regularly. One day during his visit to ADE, the Hovercraft named Nandi was ready to fly for a test flight and Menon was interested in going for a ride. Since he was interested in taking over the flights, so many objections were raised by the Group Captain and crew as the minister's safety was more important for them and they did not find it appropriate to risk his life. Besides all the objections, Menon stepped forward and went for the flight on Hovercraft and the pilot seat was honoured by none other than Kalam himself.

Hovercraft - Kalam with Krishna Menon

This was roughly the last session taken by Mr. Menon because after that he was replaced as the Defense minister. His replacement left Kalam in a dejected state because Menon, during the flight period, suggested

Kalam's group to design a more powerful vehicle, the idea of which dropped along with Menon and, for some reasons, the Hovercraft project was discontinued. But as always, destiny played its role and the new director of ADE, Prof. M. G. K. Menon, the then director of the Tata Institute of Fundamental Research (TFFR) at Bombay, came to a visit and desired his wish to take a ride on the same hovercraft. Kalam showed him the machine and took him to the flight which was quite satisfactory for all.

Kalam's meet with M. G. K. Menon brought major change in his life and destiny took a turn and lifted up his career. He was called to Bombay for an interview at TIFR for the post of Rocket Engineer at the Indian Committee for Space Research (INCOSPAR). There Kalam was selected for the post of rocket engineer by Dr. Vikram Sarabhai, who, for the first time, was a part

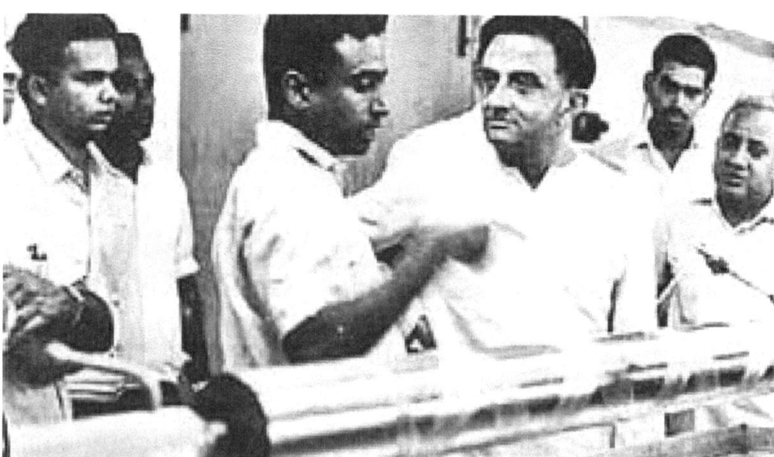

Young Dr. Abdul Kalam with Vikram Sarabhai

of the selection committee. This turn in Kalam's life changed his professional career.

Because of the advantage of Thumba (near Trivandrum in Kerela) being very close to the Earth's magnetic equator – which is quite different from the geographical equator of the Earth – INCOSPAR set up in 1962 the Thumba Equatorial Launching Station (TERLS). Its office initially was in a church which was acquired for the rocket-launching programme, with the full cooperation of the church authorities. The same church today houses the space museum of the Indian Space Research Organization (ISRO).

Under the guidance of Kalam, INCOSPAR set up the Thumba Equatorial Rocket Launching Station

Kalam and R. Aravamudan - Early days at the Thumba Equatorial Rocket Launching Station Readying equipment to be carried by a sounding rocket into the atmosphere

(TERLS) in 1962; the authorities of TERLS selected Kalam to go to US National Aeronautics and Space Administration (NASA) for six months of training on sounding rockets and their launching techniques. This was the only international training that Kalam received in his whole life. This led to Kalam's close contact with rockets and their study, the inventions of which are even seen today.

Putting his vision upon scientific research and technology development, he learned how two horses of a chariot move smoothly. Later on, he supervised the work being done on NASA's earth-orbiting satellite application.

His last training was in America, where he learned how hard-working Americans had a definite purpose

Five early recruits including Kalam (second from left) were sent to the U.S. for a training programme on sounding rockets and launching techniques

or objective for everything. His training was at Flight Test, the facility of NASA at Wallop's Island, where sounding rocket programmes are implemented. He learned how, in America, every item of work done had a definite purpose or objective and how hard-working the Americans are. There he also realized that everyone's life is full of hurdles and all fight to overcome their obstacles with determination and commitment.

At NASA's reception, a thought of dejection emerged in Kalam's mind when he saw Tipu Sultan's painting in which he was firing a rocket against the British in 1794 was there on the wall. He realized that the reason behind India's lagging was because the land where the rocket was first used as a weapon had no signs of relevance regarding this and in America, this awareness is the only reason that Americans have grown up in science and technology. The six months of his US stay made Kalam a different person. He realized that Indians were not worth their talent and their basic mindset were criticizing and complaining about one another. Indians, he felt, did not have a sense of national pride.

On his visit to the US, whatever he had learned at NASA, the time he had spent there in learning things, he had poured everything out while launching the first sounding rocket named Nike Apache, which he made at NASA. He returned to TERLS in November 1963 for the project, a joint collaboration project involving France, the USA and the USSR.

Tipu Sultan's rockets

Both Dr. Homi Bhabha and Dr. Vikram Sarabhai had clear visions about India's National Space Programme. Thus, the Space Science and Technology Centre (SSTC) came into being at Thumba in 1965. The first indigenous effort culminated in developing the Rohini Sounding Rocket (RSR). Kalam constantly had in mind what was being done while preparing sounding rockets and rocket plants. It was the revival of the technology of rockets that Tippu Sultan had initiated. It had been forgotten for about 160 years after Tipu Sultan was betrayed by his men and killed by the British in 1799.

For his work, under the guidance of Homi Bhabha and Vikram Sarabhai, on the Nike-Apache sounding rocket, Kalam was rewarded and put in charge of rocket integration and safety. With this, many laboratories in India were to be involved in the programme for developing sounding rockets. Kalam was asked to

The Nike- Apache rocket being ready for launch

interact with the Tata Institute of Fundamental Research (TIFR), National Physical Laboratory (NPL) and the Physical Research Laboratory (PRL) and also payload scientists from the U.S.A., U.S.S.R., France, Germany, Japan and other countries.

One of the featured works by Kalam and his group led R&D work in the new area of composites which was good at Structural, thermal, electrical, chemical and mechanical properties. In 1969, Kalam and his group developed the first filament winding machine. In the February of that year, the then Prime Minister, Indira Gandhi, inaugurated the machine, using high strength glass cloth laminates to build up non-magnetic payload housings for the two-stage sounding rockets, were made. Also, FRP rocket motor causing up to 360 mm in diameter were fabricated.

In 1968, Kalam was given the responsibility of the stage of SLV and was selected as the leader of the Satellite Launch Vehicle (SLV) project by Dr. Sarabhai, who headed the department of Atomic Energy after the untimely death of Dr. Homi Bhabha in a plane accident. The department of Atomic Energy led to the establishment of the Indian Space Research Organization (ISRO). Kalam was given the responsibility of the fourth stage of SLV.

Prof. Curien, who was in charge of the French Diamond Rocket Programme, was called up to Thumba by Dr. Sarabhai with a view in mind of collaboration in the space field with France. Prof. Curien was quite impressed by the work of Kalam and approached Dr. Sarabhai with a proposal to see if Kalam and his group would be able to make the fourth stage of the French Rocket.

Once in 1969, Dr. Sarabhai proposed to Kalam the development of a Rocket-Assisted Take-Off (RATO) system for military aircraft and took Kalam to Tilpat range on the outskirts of Delhi to have a view of a Russian

RATO. His motive was to create a similar RATO in India in 18 months with the help of Russian motors. For the discussion on this matter, Dr. Sarabhai called Kalam early in the morning and the appointment of the meeting was fixed at near about 3:30 a.m. at hotel Ashoka in New Delhi. Such a meeting at an early hour of the day was quite common for Dr. Sarabhai as he spent most of his time on his work rather than on his sleep.

As per the time period suggested by Dr. Sarabhai, Kalam agreed to work accordingly and Dr. Sarabhai fixed up a breakfast meeting with the then prime minister Indira Gandhi over this announcement. Soon after the meeting, all the newspapers and media were flooded with the headlines of the same announcement. Now, the country's pride was on the shoulders of Kalam and his team. Kalam decided on an FRP body for the RATO

A. P. J. Abdul Kalam with Prime Minister Indira Gandhi

system and to make use of composites propellant. During this period, Dr. Sarabhai came out with a ten-year plan for space research in India. It clearly showed the vision of Dr. Sarabhai as it emphasized self-reliance and the development of indigenous technologies.

Soon after this announcement, the other field of work they took upon was the development of the Missile Panel in the Ministry of Defence. The committee was headed by Group Captain Narayana, who headed DRDL at Hyderabad, and, of course, Kalam himself. The two used to have long discussions regarding missiles and other military weapons or product systems. The basic idea behind this was to go for indigenous systems rather than focus on importing hardware required for the defence services.

Kalam was obsessed with the development of RATO. Every moment was crucial as the work on Satellite Launch Vehicle (SLV) was also in progress. The work on the design and development of missiles by DRDL at Hyderabad and the meetings of the Missile Panel also speeded up. Things were going well until Kalam came back after attending a meeting on December 30, 1971, at Trivandrum.

On his return, he was informed about the sad demise of his mentor, Dr. Sarabhai, due to a heart attack early in the morning. Kalam felt alone as he was very much attached to Dr. Sarabhai in his working years. Dr. Sarabhai had played an important role in moulding his confidence and knowledge of Kalam and refraining from his professional career. Therefore, the passing away of his mentor made Kalam work harder and fulfill the dream of Dr. Sarabhai and give him tribute through his work. Kalam did not only say but also paid his devotion to the work, the result of which was seen ten months later when the RATO project was successfully tested.

This was the only way Kalam could get over his sorrow and anguish after Dr. Sarabhai's death. Not only this, TERLS, SSTC, Rocket Propellant Plant, the Rocket Fabrication Facility and the Propellant Fuel Complex were merged and named Vikram Sarabhai Space Centre (VSSC).

Kalam was never in favour of solo work performance while doing complex projects. He, as a leader, always preferred joining and gathering more people in the group to complete the task. But what he focused on was

Abdul Kalam celebrating the moment

coordination and teamwork, which are the key points of every team/ group and the leader himself will head the team.

Under the guidance of the leader Prof. H. G. K. Menon, Prof. Satish Dhawan was made the Director of the Indian Institute of Science at Bangalore and was assigned the head of ISRO. Meanwhile, Kalam was appointed as the project manager of SLV and Dr. Brahm Prakash guided Kalam that patience, tolerance and calmness were required to handle big projects like SLV. Being the project manager, handling complex projects was a great challenge for Kalam as he never dealt with such projects earlier and alongside at VSSC teamwork and co-operation also needed to be created and maintained.

A. P. J. Abdul Kalam is seen with then Space Chief Satish Dhawan

The industrial base of India was nowhere as broad or deep as it is today. With and under the guidance of Dr. Brahm Prakash, Director of VSSC and Prof. Dhawan, chairman of ISRO, Kalam and his well-trained team's determination, creativity and excellent teamwork led to the rise of young engineers in their early twenties or thirties.

Dr. Kalam with Satish Dhawan and Dr. Brahm Prakash

More or less at the same time, DRDO began developing a surface-to-air missile (SAM), similar to the Russian SA- 2. The DRDO project, code-named DEVIL, was sanctioned in February 1972 and it was entrusted to DRDL, Hyderabad, headed by Air Cdr. Narayanan was a dynamic person who wanted to get results fast at any cost.

Kalam was such a personality who designated all his time to his work. He knew that to achieve something unique and remarkable, one has to sacrifice his personal life and cope-up with the time demanded by his teammates and his goal. He used to communicate freely with his colleagues and welcome every constructive idea or suggestion that came from them. He used to spend a lot of time communicating and discussing things as he was a firm believer that this process helps in achieving better results.

Dr. Kalam sharing his thoughts

Moreover, the team got major help and support from Dr. Brahm Prakash, both morally and financially. Being the project leader, Kalam never bound his mates with his views and led his team (especially the youngsters) to work freely with innovative thoughts, which somehow led to better results. He had to keep somehow himself updated on new upcoming knowledge, which also demanded proper time management. In Prof. Dhawan, the chairman of ISRO and Secretary of the Department of Space (DoS), Kalam found a very knowledgeable person. The period took a setback on August 10, 1979, when the first experimental launch of SLV-3 proved to be unsuccessful. Everyone was in a dejected state, but especially for Kalam, it was heartbreaking. But by God's grace, his supporters, Dr. Brahm Prakash and Prof. Dhawan, never let him feel discouraged. So, they encouraged him to give the projects continuous trials unless and until he succeeds. So, after analyzing the cause of failure, a second attempt was made on July 18, 1980, and no doubt it was a grand success. So, all those who left their faith were now on top of the world. Kalam for his achievement was honoured not only by the scientific community but also by the Government of India.

This success of Kalam created a smell of jealousy towards which Kalam was very sensitive. But luckily, his 20 years of hardworking experience was now required by DRDL at Hyderabad. So, he received a call from there very soon and Kalam left for Hyderabad in the early eighties. On June 1, 1982, Kalam joined Defence Research and Development Organization (DRDO) in Hyderabad. At that time, Dr. Raja Ramanna was the scientific advisor who was a very dynamic person and had earned a reputation as a knowledgeable metallurgist and a good administrator. Besides having knowledge of the ongoing work at

DRDL, he preferred to have a detailed discussion of the work prior to beginning his role. He remembered what Dr. Sarabhai used to do at Thumba, how he used to invite experts from different windows in order to have complete knowledge about the project. He very well used his 20 years of work experience at Thumba along with the teachings of Dr. Sarabhai while executing greater projects like SLV-3.

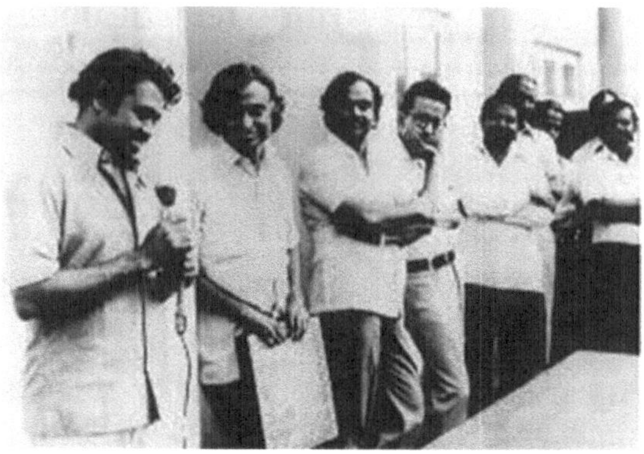

A. P. J. Abdul Kalam at DRDL, HBD.

After the final discussion, a project with a time frame of 12 years and an estimated expenditure of around Rs. 3900 million was drawn up and presented to R. Venkataraman, who luckily was the President of India and was remarked for his knowledge and understanding. Since Kalam was very much interested in this project, he was assigned the task to present the project in the meeting in New Delhi, which was attended by the Defence Minister and three other chiefs, Dr. Arunachalam and other official heads upon the design and the layout of the project.

Kalam, who once had played a crucial role in the design and development of SLV-3, which was launched on July 18, 1980, was now taking up the charge of IGMDP at DRDL, which was a more complex and difficult project.

The atmosphere in the eighties DRDL was similar to that at Thumba during the sixties and seventies. Kalam's best time was the ten years that he had spent working at DRDL while executing the IGMDP. He wholeheartedly devoted his strength, knowledge, experience and all that he could to make IGMDP a grand success. He took out his own time to select talented scientists from the best institutes and centres who were allotted the work for the project. Not only the hands but also some major institutions and organizations were called upon for their

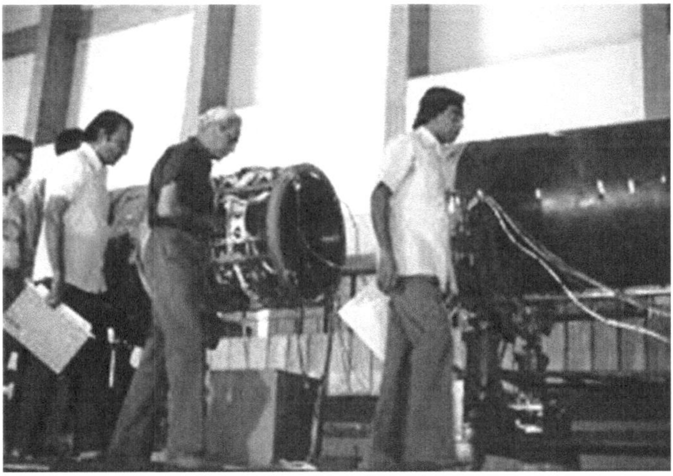

Dr. Brahm Prakash inspecting SLV-3 in its final phase of integration. He helped Abdul Kalam deal with subsequent frustrations in its launching and consoled him when he was at its lowest ebb

help, support and collaboration. Kalam's experience at Thumba helped him overtake the responsibility of this complex and challenging project in India.

A site had to be selected for the missile flight trials. It was finally decided to select Balasore in Orissa state as the Interim Test Range (ITR), an independent establishment to be ready by December 1986.

Meanwhile, Research Centre Imarat (RCI), a high technological centre, was established in the Imarat Kancha area near DRDL to work on the sixth project that was added to the five missiles of IGMDP.

In September 1983, the Defence Minister visited to take a first-hand look and view of the progress of IGMDP. He was satisfied with the progress and offered full support to the workers.

Abdul Kalam and Indira Gandhi at DRDL

On hearing this good news, the then Prime Minister, Indira Gandhi, paid a visit to DRDL.

Her speech and remarks boosted the workers' morale. She was promised the date of 'June 1987' for the first test flight of the missile. All the management techniques were arranged in India itself. Dr. Arunachalam carried out the full-fledged status review on September 27, 1984.

The approach was used to bring in 12 Academic institutions, 30 DRDO laboratories, many CSIR laboratories, ISRO and many other Industries. More than 50 professors and 100 research scholars in various academic institutions were working on missile-related R&D problems. Campus interviews were speedily organised to recruit about 300 young talented engineers. Speedy execution went side by side to pursue excellence, as Prime Minister Indira Gandhi had advised.

Rajiv Gandhi, the successor of Indira Gandhi, visited the DRDL on August 3, 1987, after the unfortunate assassination of Indira Gandhi. Till August, a good and satisfactory amount of success could be seen in the compilation of the work for building the Missile Technology Research Centre at Imarat Kancha. Rajiv Gandhi laid the foundation stone of RCI and encouraged all to go ahead with IGMDP.

Kalam, the captain of the team, was honored for the success of the IGDMP, who headed the DRDL department for around 10 years and was then called upon to the department of Defence R&D as a scientific advisor to the Defence Minister in July 1992.

Abdul Kalam having food with his mates

Despite various high-ranking engineers and scientists, Kalam had done a commendable job as the head. He always had many projects working altogether in his hand, but his aim was not to let any of them suffer any loss or damage due to negligence. These projects included IGMDP and Light Combat Aircraft (LCA) and the Pilotless Target Aircraft (PTA) project.

Kalam's humanitarian nature is seen when he stood forward to work for the destitute in the country who face problems while paying for bigger treatments. He set up (SBMT) i.e. Society of Biomedical Technology, with the main objective to bring together medical professionals and DRDO scientists and engineers to work on various products that the commoner needs but cannot afford. The orthotic appliances got available at the one-third price of imported ones.

This was very much known that the cases of heart disease are much higher in our country than in the US, but people cannot afford its treatment. To make it available, the noted cardiologist Dr. Somaraju of Hyderabad, along with Kalam, developed a metallic stent called 'Kalam – Raju stent', which got available at around Rs. 15000 in contrast to the foreign cost which was between Rs. 50000 to Rs. 75000. Dr. Somuraju also promoted the Cardiovascular Technology Institute, which according to him, "aims at developing cost-effective indigenous substitutes for imported consumables".

Abdul Kalam discussing cost effective medical facilities

An extensive techno-medical study was made in 1994 by the Society for Biomedical Technology (SBMT) to benchmark the different types of stents available in the markets, broadly classified as tubular and coil stents. Detailed experimental and clinical studies on three stents of either type have provided the necessary benchmark. This has been made the basis for the development of indigenous stents patented as Kalam-Raju stents.

Kalam-Raju stent (K-R) Stent led to the crash of prices of imported coronary stents in the Indian market by more than 50%. For this historical effort, the CARE Foundation received the Defence Technology Spin-off Award in 1998.

Another event which proved that Kalam was such a caring person was during a hectic project; one of the 70 scientists working on it asked Dr. Kalam if he could leave at 5:30 pm that evening as he had promised to take his kids to an exhibition. Dr. Kalam permitted him. However, the scientist got busy with the work only to realize that it was 8:30 pm. When he looked for his boss, he wasn't there. Guilty for having disappointed his kids, he returned home only to find that his kids were not there. When he asked his wife where they were, she replied, "You don't know? Your manager came here at 5:15 pm and took the children to the exhibition." when Dr. Kalam noticed him working hard at 5 pm, he thought to himself that this person would not leave work, but if he had promised his children, they should enjoy the exhibition. So he, the boss, took the lead and took them there!

Abdul Kalam loved spending time with kids

Along with this Kalam with his full determination, commitment and hard work came up with India's first satellite launch vehicle (SLV-3) and became the father of the successful Integrated Guided Missile Development Programme of India (IGMDP).

SLV-3 on launch

Kalam had a keen interest in the defence and space arena and even involved himself in India's Missile Programme. After working for two decades in the Indian Space Research Organization (ISRO), Kalam, being the chief executive at IGMDP, developed some of the indigenous missiles at DRDO. He was responsible for developing Agni and Prithvi missiles and for the upbringing of technologies through the networking of multiple institutions. With such contributions of Kalam in missile technology, he was honoured with the title "Missile man of India". Kalam gave the opportunity of launching IGMDP, including short-range Prithvi, medium Agni, long-range missiles named Trishul, Akash, anti-tank missile Nag.

The lead of 'Trishul' was given to Commodore S. R. Mohan; for 'Agni' it was given to MIT scholar R. N. Agarwal; for 'Nag' it was given to N. R. Iyer and for 'Akash' it was given to Prahlada. Kalam very well compared his team in his work 'Wings of Fire' to "Five Pandavas", who were married to "Draupadi of positive thinking". Not only the team, Kalam even addressed his directors and their associates, namely Sundaram, V. K Saraswat, Prahlada and others in a jolly manner as "funny guys". From large public firms to small private sector suppliers, Kalam's task was to inspire and monitor these 20 institutions.

When Kalam was appointed as the chief at DRDO, the working content in terms of missiles was only 30 per cent. But Kalam, as per his capability, assured the government of achieving a greater target than 30 per cent, which, according to him, should be around 70 per cent. Since the technologies were limited, it took 15 years to develop them and therefore, "By the time Kalam retired, DRDO achieved 50 per cent indigenization", Aatre said. In 2008, IGMDP wound up as a great success. "Nag ad Trishul may not have achieved much, but the Agni, Prithvi and the Akash are successful. In fact, Agni is a major deterrent….."

Prithvi on launch

While he was working on a construction project with DRDO, he asked the team what would they do to ensure security around a certain building. The team lead suggested: "Broken glass on the walls." The former

Agni on launch

President was quick to turn down the suggestion. He said, "The birds cannot perch on the wall. Think of something else." A politician who thought about birds as much as he did about people.

As per the commitment made by Government, a good amount of funds was raised to build a futuristic centre to work for the advanced technologies. In the Missile years, Kalam's major achievement was the establishment of the Research Centre Imarat (RCI) near DRDL. His keen interest in and towards the environment was again witnessed when he emerged from RCI as green area in an arid region.

Dr. Kalam was honoured with India's highest honourable degree, 'Bharat Ratna' on 25th November 1997, for his most outstanding efforts and devotion towards Indian Defence and Science. He was also honoured with the 'Indira Gandhi Award' for national integration in October 1998.

Kalam's intelligence gave way to India's first nuclear test at the time when Atal Bihari Vajpayee headed the government. Vajpayee was very interested in going with the test in 1996 and informed the government and the officials about the same. But due to some political instability, he put his plan to rest. Luckily, after two years, he once again got the opportunity as he came back to power and hence gave the green signal to go with the first nuclear test at Pokhran, which ended on a successful note.

Dr. Kalam with Atal Bihari Vajpayee

Kalam, the chief of the Defence Research and Development Organization, under whose guidance the nuclear test at Pokhran-II tests took place, had stated that the testing was a " defining moment" in the country's history. On May 15, 2015, Kalam tweeted that

"Today, I remember the hot day of 1998 at Pokhran: 53°C. When most of the world was sleeping, India's nuclear era emerged."

The Bhabha Atomic Research Centre (BARC) honoured Kalam with a momento of a banyan tree bonsai which had a statue of a smiling Buddha under it. "The Buddha has smiled", was the code used by the scientists in1974 to declare that nuclear test has been successful.

Acknowledged as the driving force behind India's quest in defence technologies, former president, Dr. A. P. J. Abdul Kalam's contributions to the India's satellite programmes, guided missile projects, nuclear weapons programme and the Light Combat Aircraft (LCA) project made him earn his name in his own country as well as the countries with which he had worked with.

Kalam made significant contributions as the Project Director to develop India's first indigenous Satellite Launch Vehicle (SLV-3), which successfully injected the Rohini Satellite into the near-earth orbit in July 1980 and made India an exclusive member of the space club. Kalam was also behind the evolution of the Indian Space Research Organisation's (ISRO) launch vehicle programme, particularly the Polar Satellite Launch Vehicle (PSLV) configuration. After working for two decades in ISRO and mastering launch vehicle technologies, he took up the responsibility of developing Indigenous Guided Missiles at the Defence Research and Development Organization (DRDO) as the chief executive of the Integrated Guided Missile Development Programme (IGMDP).

Kalam would take the sole blame for losses and setbacks but gave all credit to his team when they achieved anything under his leadership. Such were the qualities of the "Missile Man."

He also gave way to self-reliance in defence systems by progressing multiple development tasks and mission projects such as Light Combat Aircraft. Kalam was one of the key figures who inspired ISRO to take up its Moon and Mars missions.

Kalam vision was very much clear not only about India's Defence Centre but also towards the normal life of the people living in the country.

"I believe that connectivity is the key to bridging the Rural-Urban divide. The core competence of the village will enable the production of competitive

Dr. Kalam in an interview

products for national and international markets. This will lead to rural enterprises, which will create jobs in villages and lead to a vibrant economy in India's hinterland. That is how prosperity will emerge in the rural environment", Kalam stated in an interview in 2008 to Wharton.

In 1998, Kalam had a clear map picture drawn in his mind of transforming less developed India into a developed society in the next 20 years. On 18th June 2002, Dr. A P J Abdul Kalam was nominated for the President of India. The counting was held on 18th July, in which Kalam was declared the winner in a one-sided contest. He was supported by both the major political parties in India, i.e. Bharatiya Janta Party (BJP) and Indian National Congress. Abdul Kalam was the third President after Dr. Zakir

Abdul Kalam as the 11th President of India

Hussain and Dr. Sarvapali Radhakrishnan and the first scientist to be elected to this post.

Right after Dr. Abdul Kalam was elected as the President, he attended an event at Kerala Raj Bhawan in Trivandrum. With the power vested in him, he could have invited any two people as the Presidential guests. Guess who he called? A roadside cobbler and the owner of a very small hotel. Dr. Kalam had spent significant time as a scientist in Trivandrum. So he invited the cobbler and the hotel owner, whom he was close to during his time in Kerala.

Kalam enumerated that a leader, especially the President of India must have five important traits in oneself:

- *The leader must have vision. Without vision, you cannot be a leader. The leader must be able to travel into an unexplored path.*
- *The leader must know how to manage success, and even more importantly, failure.*
- *The leader should have the courage to make decisions.*
- *The leader should have nobility in management. Every action of the leader should be transparent. And the leader should work with integrity.*

Dr. A. P. J. Abdul Kalam was a man of vision and, during his tenure as the President of India, had lots of achievements and contributions towards the development of the country. President Dr. Abdul

Kalam declared that India would not lag in using nuclear weapons when peace is threatened. He also concentrated on the brain drain issue and insisted Indian companies to become multinational. Not only in nuclear and aerospace engineering, Dr. Kalam took an interest in other sectors of science and technology and proposed research and development of bio-implants.

Along with his career, he was totally and wholeheartedly devoted to his family members and their concerns. Kalam held his elder brother APJ Marakia in great esteem and was full of plans to celebrate his brother's 100th birthday next year. One of the things that gave Kalam immense joy was when he helped his brother get access to the 24-hour power supply

Dr. Kalam loved spending time in reading

by installing a solar panel at their ancestral home. Dr. Kalam would always be used to calling his brother before leaving or returning from an important lecture assignment. His few personal possessions included his books, his veena, some articles of clothing, a CD player and a laptop; at his death, he left no will, and his possessions went to his eldest brother, who survived him.

Kalam continued to maintain his humble and caring nature after achieving the post of President. One such incident to be shared is - It was a cold winter night in 2003 when the convoy of President A. P. J. Abdul Kalam was entering Rashtrapati Bhawan. The President suddenly stepped out of his car creating some tense moments for his security personnel.

Abdul Kalam with his elder brother and his family

Mr. Kalam met the Indo-Tibetan Border Police (ITBP) guards at the gate and wondered why they had to brave the biting cold. He ordered heaters for the security cabins and adequate warm clothes for the guards. This was just one of the many instances that reflected the humane face of President Dr. Kalam but were never publicized, says his close aide and senior scientist V. Ponraj.

In 2006, when Mr. Kalam addressed students of St. Xavier's college in Palayamkottai and visited the Kundalkulam Nuclear Power Plant and met people at the Circuit House in Madurai, there were some incidents amounting to a breach of the President's security. This led to the suspicion of the few policemen. On returning to Delhi, Mr. Kalam directed the chief Secretary of Tamil Nadu to drop action and revoke the suspicions.

"Simplicity was an inborn quality which he practised till the last. When he was the President, the palatial Rashtrapati Bhawan would have hardly two or three rooms lit after dusk. One would be his bedroom. After a long day, Mr. Kalam listened to his favorite music on an outdated two-in-one tape recorder."

Kalam, as mentioned earlier, was a man of vision and did his best for the nation not only before but also after becoming the President. He was quite motivated in all aspects but specifically when it comes to education; while his visits to institutes, he asked students to develop curiosity, knowledge, thinking, hard work and perseverance to be successful not only for their own future but also for the bright future of the nation. In his

5 years of tenure, he even himself visited various educational institutes and concentrated on the smooth functioning all over India.

Kalam even set a target of interacting with 1,00,000 students during the two years after he resigned from the post of scientific advisor in 1999.

He explained, *"I feel comfortable in the company of young people, particularly high school students. Henceforth, I intend to share experiences with them, helping them ignite their imagination and preparing them to work for a developed India for which the road map is already available."*

Abdul Kalam encouraging and motivating young students

There are interesting incidents of interaction between a student and Dr. Kalam that went viral and became a source of motivation for many other students. They are as follows:

Student's question: You always give a message to dream. Tell me why to dream?

Dr. Kalam: "Dream, dream, dream. Dream transforms into thoughts. Thoughts result in action."

Question : Another boy asked "please tell me, who would be the first scientist in the world?"

Dr. Kalam: The foundation of science is questioning. Children are the source of unending questions. Hence "Child is the first scientist."

On his visit to Tezpur in Assam, a student asked him an interesting question. "Why cannot water from the Brahmaputra, which is in flood much of the time, be diverted to Rajasthan or Tamil Nadu, which are starved of water?

Dr. Kalam replied: "India Vision 2020 demands from the young that they start a great mission of connecting rivers cutting across the states."

Question : "Sir, will your Agni missiles cross the ocean and reach America?"

Dr. Kalam : "For us no country is our enemy to send Agni there. Particularly America is our friend. Agni symbolizes our strength. It shows that India has all the capabilities.'

Question : 'Sir tell us which are your favourite books that you loved and which have shaped your mind?"

Dr. Kalam : "Four books in my life have been close to my heart. I cherish reading them. The first is *'Man the Unknown'* by Alexis Carrel, a doctor turned philosopher a Nobel Laureate. This book highlights how the mind and body both have to be treated in an ailment as the two are integrated. The second book is *'Tiruvalluvar's Thirukkural'*, which provide an excellent code of life. The third is *'Light from Many Lamps'* by Lillian Eichler. It illuminates how we live and has been an invaluable guide to me. The fourth is *'Holy Quran'* a constant companion.

Addressing another gathering, one smart boy asked , "Who is our enemy?"

"Poverty" was the answer given by the audience.

The last question is "Tell me, sir, are Pakistani weapons stronger than Indian ones?"

Abdul Kalam answers, "This is a unique characteristic of our country- to belittle our capabilities. It may even be genetic! India can design, develop and produce any type of missile and any type of nuclear weapon. This is a capability that only four countries in the world have."

As the president, Dr. Kalam's office often would receive requests from youngsters for a meeting with the country's first citizen. Not only would Dr. Kalam meet the kids in his personal chambers at the Rashtrapati Bhawan, but he would also give them his precious time, listen to their ideas and provide feedback to them. On occasions, the president would follow up with such kids asking about the status of the ideas they discussed!

"Let us sacrifice our today so that our children can have a better tomorrow."

-A. P. J. Abdul Kalam

Abdul Kalam's special interaction with High School Students

To fight corruption making India the next big thing, Dr. A P. J. Abdul Kalam's initiatives involved the youth at almost every step. He launched a Facebook page to share inspiring stories and another initiative to help children give back instead of taking from society. He was the inspiration for the programme which makes the study of science immensely interesting.

He was such a humble person as when some Indian students met him during the International Space Development Conference (ISDC) in San Diego, California, in 2013, they went up to his dining table to say hello. The President, who was eating dinner, asked a student to eat from his plate. Highly surprised, he took a leaf of spinach from his salad when he insisted. "Till his day, I take it to be a leaf of inspiration from him and the best dinner I could ever imagine".

Soon after being declared that Dr. Kalam would be the next President, he visited a modest school to deliver a speech. While speaking to around 40 students, Kalam ensured the power cut didn't cause any interruption. He walked right into the middle of the crowd and asked the students to surround him. He then spoke to them with his bare voice and delivered, like always, an inspiring keynote.

President Kalam was also known to write his own 'Thank You' cards. Being one of the most humble and generous men, President Kalam was known to sign his own 'Thank You' cards. One instance is when Quora user Naman Narain drew a sketch of Dr. Kalam and sent it to the President. To his surprise, the President sent him a 'Thank You' card, with a short handwritten message personalized with his signature.

One of the inspiring speech that he shared with his students and teacher when he had met them is as follows….

"It doesn't matter who I am, I will work, work and work. All the forces of the universe will also assist me. I will achieve what I dream. Even reaching any part of our Galaxy, I am delighted to participate in the inaugural ceremony of the Silver Jubilee Celebrations of Ernad Muslim Educational Association (EMEA) and interact with students and faculty members of EMEA College of Art and Science. I congratulate the Principal, Teachers, Students and Staff of this college, both present and past and also all those who have contributed to building

the robust framework for shaping young minds and developing them to blossom as enlightened citizens of the nation. My Greetings to all during your Silver Jubilee Celebrations. While I am with you, I would like to recall one incident which occurred during my childhood (Age 10). Each day when I returned home from school in the evening, my father would go to namaz. And my mother would be performing namaz and look angelic. After Thakbhir position, she will recite two suras from Holy Quran. One starts with Alhamdhu and the other "Lakkum, Theenukum". One day I asked my parents what the meaning of Lakkum Theenukum is? My mother, in a graceful voice, recited the sura "Lakkum TheenukumValiyatheen" that is the end of the sura Alkhafeerun. My father said, "it means everyone follows a path. He or she who decides the path is accountable for the actions". My father, who was Imam of the local mosque, elaborated, "my son, I meet my friends quite often as you would have seen me with Pakshi Lakshmana Shastrigal and Rev Father Bodal." Pakshi Lakshmana Shastrigal was a great Hindu devotee and the head priest of Rameswaram Siva Temple and Rev Father Bodal had built our Island's first church. In my childhood, I was indeed blessed to hear the discussion of the great three personalities. At least once a week, they met and discussed the integration of thoughts from the Holy Quran, Holy Bible and Bhagavad Gita. From the essence of their saying, I learnt, whatever religion you are, the path you select will lead you to bliss based on your good action. The topic I have selected for the discussion is "No youth today need to fear about the future.

Friends, today India have a mission of transforming itself into a developed nation with a value system. This is a great challenge. This can be achieved through our youth's power. Youth has got the power of ideas, ambition, enthusiasm and ability. This resource of the youth is an important building block for transforming India into a developed nation. Friends, I would like to assert that "No youth today need to fear about the future". How? If you have an aim in life, realize that spent time cannot be recovered; hence the precious time has to be used for achieving the goal, having the confidence to win, having the confidence to defeat the problems and succeed and have a righteous heart, you will definitely succeed in all your missions. The teachers in student's life, what they can give? In an integrated way, it can be said that any enlightened human being can be created by the teacher by providing two unique characteristics. One is building capacities among the students to inquire, innovate, be creative, entrepreneur and have moral leadership. Second is the development of a moral value system. The noble life practised by the teacher indeed becomes a beacon of light to the students. Let us hear the tribute given by the great teacher Albert Einstein to the teacher: "The ideals which have lighted my way, time after time, have given new course to face life cheerfully have been kindness, beauty and truth". This is the mission of a teacher. It will be a God-given gift to the student to have great teachers who can give and give the learning module and the way of a beautiful life. With these words, let me once again greet you all on the occasion of Silver Jubilee Celebrations. My best wishes to all the Students, Teachers, and Staff of EMEA College of Art and Science success in their missions of developing as enlightened citizens and actively participating in transforming India into a developed nation well before 2020."

During his tenure as a president, he was titled "People's President", assigning the Office of Profit Bill was the most challenging decision. As per article 72 of the Constitution, India empowers the President to grant pardons, suspend or commute the death sentence of the convicts, for which Kalam was criticized. Kalam acted on only one mercy plea in his year tenure as a president, rejecting the plea of the rapist Dhananjoy Chatterjee, who was later hanged. Afzal Guru, who was convicted of conspiracy in the December 2001 attack on the Indian Parliament, was sentenced to death by the Supreme Court of India in 2004. The pending action on his mercy plea resulted in him remaining on death row. In September 2003, in an interactive session in PGI Chandigarh, Kalam supported the need for Uniform Civil Code in India, keeping in view the country's population. During the end days of his tenure, he expressed his willingness to go forward for his second term elections for his post as he had a certainty of his victory in the upcoming elections in

2007. However, after two days after his decision, he changed his mindset and decided not to contest the Presidential election again, stating that he wanted to avoid involving Rashtrapati Bhawan in any political process. He did not have the support of the left parties, Shiv Sena and UPA constituents, to receive a renewed mandate.

On looking various favors as well as criticisms, he declined to contest the 2012 presidential poll. He said of his decision not to do so:

"Many, many citizens have also expressed the same wish. It not only reflects their love and affection for me and the aspiration of the people. I am really overwhelmed by this support. This being their wish, I respect it. I want to thank them for the trust they have in me."

After leaving office, Kalam became a visiting professor at the Indian Institute of Management Shillong, the Indian Institute of Management, Ahmedabad and the Indian Institute of Management Indore, an honorary fellow of the Indian Institute of Science, Bangalore, Chancellor of the Indian Institute of Space Science and Technology, Thiruvananthapuram; Professor of Aerospace Engineering at Anna University; and an adjunct at many other academic and research institutions across India. He taught information technology at the International Institute of Information Technology, Hyderabad, at Banaras Hindu University and Anna University.

"Based on my visits to all the states and Union Territories in the country and 16 countries in Asia, Europe and Africa as a President and meeting over 1.5 million youth, I realize that all the youth, irrespective of which country they belong to, aspire to live in a peaceful, happy, prosperous and safe nation. What does it mean? It means that economic prosperity alone is not sufficient. It has to be complemented with the value systems and our five-thousand-year-old civilization heritage which has genetically shaped the Indian people.

I believe, when the nation is progressing towards economic development, it is also essential to build education with a value system drawn from our Civilization heritage. The good human life comes out of the way we live; we may have many problems. But the billion people have the connectivity which gives us the united strength."

-A. P. J. Abdul Kalam

A. P. J. Abdul Kalam always used to say that he would like to be remembered as a teacher. When he became the President of India in 2002, he made no compromise on his penchant for teaching. He grabbed every single opportunity to teach his students, especially children, wherever he went. Administering a pledge on national development to the youth was his passion. On the occasion of 'Teacher's Day' on September 5, 2013, the former president said: "If people remember me as a good teacher, that will be the biggest honour for me."

Not only this, minutes before his end came on July 27, 2015, Mr. Kalam was teaching his students at the Indian Institute of Management, Shillong.

"Teaching is a noble profession that shapes the character, caliber and future of an individual...youth have a dream and have pain. The pain comes out of their dream; they want to live in a prosperous, happy and peaceful India. This student environment ignites me and leads me to interact with young minds." Dr. Kalam said in an interview.

Once during an event, the country's first bachelor president, Kalam, refused to sit on a chair designated for him at convocation at BHU because the chairs were larger than the other chairs! No doubt, another chair was made available immediately for the honourable former President.

At the Indian Institute of Technology, Hyderabad Dr. A. P. J. Abdul Kalam gave one of his finest speeches where he portrayed his own vision for India. It goes like....

"I have three visions for India. In 3000 years of our history, people from all over the world have invaded us, captured our lands, conquered our minds. From Alexander onwards, The Greeks, the Turks, the Moguls, the Portuguese, the British, the French, and the Dutch came and looted us, took over what was ours. Yet we have not done this to any other nation. We have not conquered any other nation. We have not conquered anyone. We have not grabbed their land, culture, or history and tried to

Abdul Kalam delivering his speech at Indian Institute of Technology(IIT)

enforce our way of life on them. Why? Because we respect the freedom of others.

That is why my first vision is that of FREEDOM. I believe that India got its first vision of this in 1857, when we started the war of Independence. It is this freedom that we must protect and nurture and build on. If we are not free, no one will respect us.

My second vision for India's DEVELOPMENT, for fifty years we have been a developing nation. It is time we see ourselves as a developed nation. We are among the top 5 nations of the world in terms of GDP. We have a 10 per cent growth rate in most areas. Our poverty levels are falling. Our achievements are being globally recognized today. Yet we lack the self-confidence to see ourselves as a developed nation, self-reliant and self-assured. Isn't this incorrect?

I have a third vision. India must stand up to the world. Because I believe that unless India stands up to the world, no one will respect us. Only strength respects strength. We must be strong not only as a military power but also as an economic power. Both must go hand-in-hand. My good fortune was to have worked with three great minds. Dr. Vikram Sarabhai of the Dept. Of Space, Prof. Satish Dhawan, who succeeded him and Dr. Brahm Prakash, father of nuclear material. I was lucky to have worked with all three of them closely and consider this the great opportunity of my life.

Kalam looked forward to his four major movements keeping in mind the future of his nation. These included:

1. The what can I give movement:
   In 2012, Dr. Kalam launched the self-governed 'What Can I Give Movement' to spread the message and idea of 'giving' among the youth. And the movement strived to replace the attitude of greed and corruption that comes from the thought, "what can I take" with an attitude giving their name to the initiative.

2. Billion Beats:
   Dr. Kalam's e-paper Billion Beats, in circulation since 2007, later turned into a Facebook page on which Kalam shared his interactions with

achievers and their success stories and even shared his thoughts on developed India before the year 2020.

3. India Vision 2020:
   In 1998 Kalam put forward a countrywide plan called Technology Vision 2020, which he described as a road map for transforming India from a less-developed to a developed society in 20 years. This plan, initially a document prepared by the Technology Information, Forecasting and Assessment Council (TIFAC) of India's Department of Science and Technology under the chairmanship of Dr. A.P.J Abdul Kalam, was later elaborated on in his book, wherein he recognized five core areas "for integrated action to double the growth rate of GDP" in India. These five areas were agriculture, infrastructure, education and healthcare, information and communication technologies, critical technologies and strategic industries.

4. Igniting Minds:
   The programme, named after Dr. Kalam's bestseller, aimed to connect over one lakh Indian students, technocrats and leaders to make education in science more interesting. Started by Vijnana Bharti, Igniting minds made the leaders of the Indian scientific community digitally available for interactions, one of whom was missile man Dr. Kalam.

Abdul Kalam with his assets

Some inspire a few, and there are very rare ones who inspire an entire generation. Dr. A. P. J. Abdul Kalam was one of the very rare ones. He was a scientist, a teacher, and President of India from 2002 to 2007. He had touched so many lives and ignited so many young minds to believe in the power of thinking, knowledge, and self-belief. People admire him not for what he has given to Science but also for his unmatchable personality. There are many inspiring traits of this great leader which are as follows:

- Be Prepared…

  Life does not always follow the path we have set for it.

  Sometimes, it takes its own course and makes us follow it instead. We never know what's next.

So, always be ready for the best and the worst. Success and Failure are the two faces of the same coin. Work hard to achieve your goal and never let yourself down.

"Excellence is a continuous process not an accident."

-A. P. J. Abdul Kalam

- Be courageous and Think differently…

One of the major life lessons from A. P. J. Abdul Kalam is that you must be courageous enough to think differently. He said *"My message, especially to young people, is to have courage to think differently, courage to invent, to travel the unexplored path, courage to discover the impossible and to conquer the problems and succeed.* In a country like ours where lakhs of students are preparing and competing for that one seat of their dream in **engineering** and **medical college**, conviction and purpose with courage can only make that dream come true? It is your mind and thinking that makes all the difference here and not all those hours you've spent solving a paper! Make the best use of your mind, think differently & identify the techniques that set you apart from the rest.

"What is the secret of success? -Right Decisions.
How do you make right decisions? -Experience.
How do you gain experience? -Wrong decisions."

- A. P. J. Abdul Kalam

- Be humble...

This should top the list because everything else fails in the absence of this. Dr. Kalam always emphasized that you should never lose out on your humbleness, even if you are the head of an entire nation. Modesty has and will remain a powerful trait because where egoism fails, humbleness conquers.

The most talented son of India, A. P. J. Abdul Kalam was a patrician from humble beginnings who never forgot his own past or the grand history of his country. He inspired his country in his own humble ways. When asked how he would like to be remembered, Dr. A. P. J. Abdul Kalam responded by saying, as a 'teacher'.

"It is very easy to defeat someone,
But it is very hard to win someone."

-A. P. J. Abdul Kalam

- Have a Goal…

As mentioned earlier also, Dr. Kalam had always followed the three visions for India. First vision

FREEDOM. He believes that India got its first vision in the year 1857, India's first war of Independence.

His second vision was India's DEVELOPMENT. Dr. Kalam's Vision 2020 to transform India into a 'developed' nation focuses on five areas that need to be optimized: Infrastructure, Education and Healthcare, Information and Communication Technology, Agriculture and Food Processing, and Strategic industries like space and defence technology. And the third holy vision is that India must stand up for the world.

Without a doubt, Dr. Kalam worked really hard and contributed humongous efforts to the vision of India. He lived as an example of hard work, resilience and positive attitude, and people remember him as the most beloved president. He was known to be the "Missile Man" for his work on the development of science and technology. These values of A. P. J. Abdul Kalam are so inspirational and motivational.

"To succeed in your mission,
You must have single-minded devotion to your goal."

-A. P. J. Abdul Kalam

- Connect with People...

Even after retirement, Dr. A. P. J. Abdul Kalam, the people's president, set himself on a demanding schedule of speeches, notably in educational institutions, and had an uncanny ability to connect with various audiences. His connection with all the people at work and with the whole country are some values of A. P. J. Abdul Kalam to be emulated. He teaches people to stay connected with everyone and spread positive thoughts. He was the one who motivated everybody in the country with his inspiring speeches. He taught the youth to take responsibility and work toward development with loyalty and integrity.

"Dream is not what you see in sleep
Dream is something which doesn't let you sleep."

-A. P. J. Abdul Kalam

Dr. Kalam's inspirational life itself is a great inspiration. He was not only the leader of India. He was a leader for the whole world. The values of A. P. J. Abdul Kalam, his contributions, his vision for a stronger India and his attitude towards life are indeed inspiring.

Apart from indulging in science, technology and other innovations, whatever he had experienced through the journey of his life, he tried to pen down all the hurdles and the motivations altogether in order to encourage the youth of the society to gather courage and work together for the betterment of oneself as well as the nation.

"Writing is my love. If you love something, you find a lot of time. I write for two hours a day, usually starting at mid night; at times I start at 11."

-A. P. J. Abdul Kalam

A. P. J. Abdul Kalam, a scientist, leader, thinker, teacher and writer; he achieved remarkable success in various fields. Yet, what endeared him to so many was his dedication to the idea of a developed India, his simple and direct way of interacting with people and his deep love for his fellowmen. In "My Life", Kalam writes his life story starting from his days growing up at Rameswaram, about working on India's space and missile programmes, his years as the 11th president of India, and his life thereafter.

Full of anecdotes that demonstrate the importance of hard work, commitment, courage and innovative thinking, this autobiography is a wonderful introduction to a remarkable life. Beautifully illustrated and simply written. "My life" will inspire readers of all ages.

- 'Wings of Fire' is a biography of India's president Abdul Kalam which has been co-authored with famous Arun Tiwari, who once had worked with Kalam in the field of military defense research. As from the book itself, "this is the story of Kalam who flourished from darkness into the bright sunlight, his personal and professional effort. This is also the narrative of independent India's struggle for technological self adequacy & sovereignty in defense systems, a story as much regarding politics, as it is regarding science."

Abdul Kalam has been one of the most iconic figures of Independent. The story tells us about Kalam's rise from a humble lower-middle-class family and his narrative of India's efforts in rocketry & space technology. Segregated into four sections, the book gradually reaches for the stars – Orientation, Creation, Propitiation, and Contemplation. As a tribute to his mother and father, the book is dedicated to his parents.

This book offers an important lesson about finding success from the failures of Indian space and rocket infrastructural programs. A good presentation of the role of other renowned scientists in moulding our country's future, this book has the influence and power to motivate a person to stand out in life. "Wings of Fire" is a unique model of accomplishing one's goals while fulfilling the promise to its country.

- Kalam even described his 15 years of spiritual journey in his final book, *Transcendence: My Spiritual Experience.* Pramukh Swamiji, through a chance meeting, became friend to one of India's most eminent citizens, the eleventh president of India, Dr. A. P. J. Abdul Kalam, and together they created an unparalleled fellowship of science and spirituality. In Transcendence, Dr. Kalam, with his co-author and pupil Arun Tiwari, maps a journey of self-realization reflected in the compassionate eyes of Pramukh Swamiji, painting a delightfully open-hearted portrait of the fusion of spirituality, science and leadership. He describes how his path has been illuminated by Swamiji's words and his inspirational, loving presence.

Through the life of Pramukh Swamiji and the transnational work of the BAPS Swaminarayan Sanstha, Dr. Kalam traces the contemporary concerns of the Indian diaspora across the world and the emerging Indian identity of a capable, right-thinking and hardworking people. Drawing from the lives of great scientists and creative leaders, Transcendence captures the essence of all religions. It is a fountain of inspiration and a treasury of wisdom as it is a tribute to the multi-faith, pluralistic Indian society.

- Moreover, A. P. J. Abdul Kalam, the 11th President of India dedicated his book, 'Ignited Minds' to a class 12th girl, Snehal Thakkar, who had impressed him with her response to poverty. He also invited her personally for the swearing-in at Rashtrapati Bhawan, when he took over to the President of India on July 25, 2002.

Kalam, for his tremendous contributions to the field of science and technology as well as for his writings which played a major role in evoking the minds of the youth, had received various awards and recognition from the Government of India and several political parties. His 79th birthday was recognized as 'World

Kalam at his final stage

Student's Day' by United Nations. He also received honorary doctorates from 48 universities.

To begin with, he was honoured with 'Padma Bhushan' and 'Padma Vibhushan' in 1981 and 1990, respectively. In 1994 he was given the 'Distinguished Fellow' award by the Institute of Directors (India). He was honoured with both 'Bharat Ratna' and 'Indira Gandhi Award for National Integration' in 1997. He received 'Veer Savarkar Award' and 'Ramanujan Award' in 1998 and 2000. In 2007, he received 'An Honorary Doctorate of Science' from the University of Wolverhampton and 'King Charles II Medal' from the Royal Society, UK. 'Doctor of Engineering' was given to Kalam in 2008. In 2009, he was honoured with the 'International Von Karman Wings Award' from the California Institute of Technology, USA;

‘Hoover Medal’ from ASME Foundation, USA and ‘Honorary Doctorate’ from Oakland University. He was awarded ‘A Doctor of Engineering’ from the University of Waterloo in 2010. In 2012, Simon Fraser University honoured Kalam with ‘Doctor of Laws (Honoris causa)’. He received ‘A Doctor of Science’ from Edinburgh University, the UK, in 2014.

Following his death, Dr. A. P. J. Abdul Kalam received numerous various tributes. The Tamil Nadu state government announced that his birthday, 15th October, would be observed across the state as “Youth Renaissance Day”; the state government further instituted the “Dr. A. P. J. Abdul Kalam Award”, constituting an 8-gram gold medal, a certificate and Rs. 5,00,000. The award will be awarded annually on Independence Day, beginning in 2015, to the residents of the state with achievements in promoting scientific growth, the humanities or the welfare of the students.

Kalam Award for ISRO Scientist: Chief Minister Jayalalithaa presented the first A. P. J. Abdul Kalam Award to Indian Space Research Organization (ISRO) scientist N. Valarmathi, who led the team that successfully launched Radar Imaging Satellite RISAT-1 in 2012. The daughter of a government employee from Aliyalur, Ms Valarmathi, was presented a certificate, a cheque for Rs. 5 lacs and an 8-gram gold coin at the Independence Day function at Fort St. George. Ms

Jayalalithaa announced the award in memory of former president A. P. J. Abdul Kalam.

Kalam was nominated for the 'MTV Youth Icon of the Year' Award in 2003 and in 2006. In the year 2011, in Hindi Film '*I am Kalam*', Kalam is portrayed as an extremely positive influence to a poor but bright Rajasthani boy named Chhotu, who renames himself Kalam in honor of his idol.

"If you want to shine like a sun first burn like a sun."

-A.P.J Abdul Kalam

Several educational and scientific institutions and other locations were renamed or named in honor of Kalam:

- ❖ An agricultural college at Kishanganj, Bihar was renamed the 'Dr. Kalam Agricultural College Kishanganj', by Bihar State Government.
- ❖ Uttar Pradesh Technical University (UPTU) was renamed 'A. P. J. Abdul Kalam Technical University' by Uttar Pradesh state government.
- ❖ On October 15, 2015, Defence Research Development Organization's (DRDO's) Missile Complex, which was also considered to be the brain child of Dr. Kalam, in Hyderabad was renamed as 'Dr. A. P. J. Abdul Kalam Missile Complex' on the occasion of his 84th birth anniversary.
- ❖ The Assam government set up a Assam Centre for Innovation named after A. P. J. Abdul Kalam.

- Wheeler Island, a national missile test site in Odisha, was renamed Abdul Kalam Island in September 2015.

"Don't read success stories, you will only get a message. Read failure stories, you will get some ideas to get success."

-A. P. J. Abdul Kalam

Kalam sharing his quotes of encouragement

As a leader whose life inspired and will continue to inspire the Indians, some of the famous quotes by Kalam are:

- You have to dream before your dreams can come true.
- If a country is to be corruption free and become a nation of beautiful minds. I strongly feel there are three key societal members who can make a

difference. They are the father, the mother and the teacher.

- Look at the sky. We are not alone. The whole universe is friendly to us and conspires only to give the best to those who dream and work.
- Teaching is a very noble profession that shapes the character, caliber and future of an individual. If people remember me as a good teacher, that will be the biggest honor for me.
- Never stop fighting until you arrive at your destined place, that is, the unique you. Have an aim in life, continuously acquire knowledge, work hard, and have perseverance to realize the great life.
- Man needs his difficulties because they are necessary to enjoy success.
- Excellence is a continuous process and not an accident.
- We should not give up and we should not allow the problem to defeat us.
- Don't take rest after your first victory because if you fail in second, more lips are waiting to say that your first victory was just luck.
- If you want to shine like a sun first burn like a sun.
- Failure will never overtake me if my determination to succeed is strong enough.
- All of us do not have equal talent. But, all of us have an equal opportunity to develop our talents.

- ❖ Without your involvement you can't succeed. With your involvement you can't fail.
- ❖ For great men, religion is a way of making friends; small people make religion a fighting tool.
- ❖ If we are not free, no one will respect us.
- ❖ Science is global. Einstein's equation $E=mc^2$ has to reach everywhere. Science is a beautiful gift to humanity. We should not distort it. Science does not discriminate between multiple races.
- ❖ Be more dedicated to making solid achievements than in running after swift but synthetic happiness.
- ❖ Love your job but don't love your company, because you may not know when your company stops loving you.
- ❖ Life is a difficult game. You can win it only by retaining your birthright to be a person.
- ❖ Failure will never overtake me if my definition to succeed is strong enough.
- ❖ Great dreams of great dreamers are always transcended.
- ❖ For me, there is no such thing as a negative experience.
- ❖ Climbing to the top demand strength, whether it is to the top of Mount Everest or to the top of your career.
- ❖ Let not thy winged days be spent in vain. When once gone no gold can buy them back.
- ❖ To achieve any success, you have to first control your sense and when this is combined with vision you can achieve any goal.

- ❖ I was willing to accept what I couldn't change.
- ❖ I am not handsome but I can give my hand to someone who needs help. Because beauty is required in the heart, not in face.
- ❖ Winners are not those who never fail but those who never quit.

Missile Man of India

It was a setting that had defined his life, first as a scientist and then as India's 11th President. It was also one that sums up his final moments. The man who redefined the Presidency crafted a political idiom that spoke to children in a country growing young, whose rise from a lab to the scientific establishment to Rashtrapati Bhavan had earned him the title 'Missile Man', the eighty-three-year-old former President, Dr. A. P. J. Abdul Kalam breathed his last in Shillong on Monday night. He was at the Indian Institute of Management for a course on livable planet Earth when he suddenly suffered a massive heart attack. He was immediately taken to the hospital. Although doctors struggled for almost 45 minutes to save his life, but couldn't save him.

In Kalam, the presidency acquired a new face: the bachelor and vegetarian who played the Rudra Veena also became the first Indian President to fly a Sukhoi jet, travel in a submarine, and visit the high altitude battleground in Siachen. However, it was Kalam's ability to communicate with children and youth during lectures, seminars and public interactions that became a hallmark of his life, even after his presidency.

Kalam as a well-known scientist

Kalam's body was airlifted in an Indian Air Force helicopter from Shillong to Guwahati, from where it was flown to New Delhi on the morning of 28th July in an Air Force C-130J Hercules. The flight landed at Palam Air Base that afternoon. It was received by the President, the Prime Minister, Chief Minister of Delhi Arvind Kejriwal and other senior officers laid the wreaths on Kalam's body as a mark of tribute. At 10 Rajaji Marg, the public and various other dignitaries paid homage, including former Prime Minister Dr. Manmohan Singh, Congress president and vice-president Sonia Gandhi and Rahul Gandhi, followed by Chief Minister of Uttar Pradesh Akhilesh Yadav. Pranab Mukherjee, the man who occupied the chair that Kalam did from 2002 to 2007, stated," Dr. Kalam was a people's President during his lifetime and will remain so even after his death."

On 29th July, in afternoon, Kalam's body was taken to Madurai Airport, wrapped in the Indian flag. His body was received by the three service chiefs and national and state dignitaries, including cabinet ministers Manohar

Tribute to Kalam on his death

Parrikar, Venkaiah Naidu, Pon Radhakrishnan and Governors of Tamil Nadu and Meghalaya, K. Rosaiah and V. Shanmuganathan.

From there, Kalam's body was taken to his hometown i.e. Rameswaram, where his body was displayed in an open area in front of the local bus station to allow the public to pay their final homage.

On 30th July 2015, the former President was laid to rest at Rameswaram's Pei Karumba Ground with full state honours. Over 3,50,000 people attended the last rites, including the Prime Minister, the Governor of Tamil Nadu, followed by the Chief ministers of Karnataka, Kerala and Andhra Pradesh.

Dr. A. P. J. Abdul Kalam's death had seen an outpouring of grief and tributes to the former Indian President not only from the nation as well as from other countries too. The Government of India declared a seven-day state mourning period as a mark of respect. PM Narendra Modi said, "Dr. Kalam's death is a great loss to the scientific community. He took India to great heights. He showed the way." Former Prime Minister Dr. Manmohan Singh, who served as the prime minister under Kalam, said, "Our country has lost a great human being who made phenomenal contributions to promoting self-reliance in defence technologies. I worked very closely with Dr. Kalam as a Prime Minister and I greatly benefitted from his advice as the President of our country. His life and work will be remembered for generations to come."

Indian space agency chief A.S. Krishna Kumar termed the sudden demise of Kalam a tremendous loss to the country. "It is very saddened to know that Kalam is no more. He was such a great personality and a gentleman. No words to express." Kumar said.

The Bhutanese government ordered the country's flag to be half bowed to mourn Kalam's death and lit 1000 butter lamps in homage. Bangladesh Prime minister Sheikh Hasina described Kalam as "a rare combination of a great statesman, acclaimed scientist, and a source of inspiration to the young generation of South Asia" and termed his death "an irreparable loss to India and beyond". In a special gesture, Secretary-General of the United Nations, Ban Ki-Moon, visited the Permanent Mission of India to the UN and signed the condolence book placed following his death. "The outpouring of grief worldwide is a testament to the respect and inspiration he has garnered during and after his presidency. The UN joins the people of India in sending our deepest condolences for this great statesman."

Moreover, United Nations Organization (U.N.O) had declared his birthday (October 15th) as 'World's Students day'. It was back in 2010 that United Nations had decided to honour this great man. Even Google bids farewell to Dr. A. P. J. Abdul Kalam in its own way. A black ribbon on its home page was placed right below its search tab reads 'In the memory of Dr. A. P. J. Abdul Kalam' during mouse over. Dr. A. P. J. Abdul Kalam National Memorial is a memorial built in the memory of late President Kalam at Rameshwaram, Tamil Nadu, India. Prime Minister Narendra Modi inaugurated the Memorial on July 27th, 2017. It was built by Defence Research & Development Organization (DRDO).

"Goodbyes should be short, really short."

-A. P. J. Abdul Kalam

"The lives of great men remind us, we can make our lives sublime, and departing, leave behind us, footprints on the sands of time."

-William Wordsworth

Former President APJ Abdul Kalam wasn't around when Wordsworth wrote these lines. Had both the men belonged to the same age then these lines would have surely been written for.

CHRONOLOGY

Since the life history of our 11th President is an incredible and inspiring journey, let us sum up his most important events and years in the chronological manner.

YEARS	DESCRIPTION
1931	Avul Pakir Jainulabdeen Abdul Kalam was born on October 15, in Rameshwaram, Tamil Nadu, to Jainulabdeen, a boat owner, and a homemaker Ashiamma; Kalam went to Ramanathapuram Schwartz Matriculation School and worked from an early age to supplement the family income.
1954	Kalam graduated in physics from Saint Joseph's College, Tiruchirappalli; he moved to Madras to pursue further education after graduation.
1960	Kalam completed his degree in Aeronautical Engineering from Madras Institute of Technology (MIT) and joined the Defense Research and Development Organisation (DRDO) as a scientist.
1969	Kalam moved to the Indian Space Research Organization (ISRO) where he helmed India's first Satellite Launch Vehicle (SLV-3).
1970	Kalam headed Project Devil and Project Valiant, which developed ballistic missiles from the technology of the SLV programme.

1980	Kalam led India's efforts to enter the space club by putting the Rohini satellite in Earth's orbit with the first indigenous SLV-3.
1980-1990	As the chief of the Integrated Guided Missile Development Programme, he was credited with the development and operationalisation of Agni and Prithvi missiles
1981	Kalam received the Padma Bhushan for his contribution to the field of science and technology.
1990	Honored with Padma Vibhushan, India's second highest Civilian honor
1992-1999	Kalam was appointed as the Chief Scientific Advisor to the Prime Minister and the Secretary of the DRDO.
1997	Honored with the Bharat Ratna, India's highest Civilian honor, for his contribution to the scientific research and modernization of defense technology in India.
1998	India conducted the Pokhran II nuclear tests in May with Dr. Kalam being one of the forces behind its success.
1999-2001	Served as the Principal Scientific Advisor to the Government of India.
2002-2007	Kalam was elected as the 11th President of India succeeding K.R. Narayanan; During his five years in the office, he was fondly called ' The People's President'.
2012	Kalam launched the 'What Can I Give Movement', a programme for the Indian youth aimed at defeating corruption.
2015	Kalam passed away at the age of 83, after collapsing because of a cardiac arrest while delivering a lecture at IIM Shillong on July 27.

Acknowledgement

I am grateful to God for giving me the opportunity and courage to do, knowledge to understand, and a strong will to attempt and take over the task of highlighting the important events, dates, incidents and contributions of Dr. A.P. J. Abdul Kalam.

I would like to express my gratitude and regards to one and all who helped me through the journey of this writing and always be supportive.

I would like to thank all my readers to read this book. You are my real source of inspiration. Your support, views and recommendations encourage me to improve and keep on writing.

-Savneet Kaur